with a brief description and an assessment of their potential for success:

Content Page

Business growth can be beneficial for a variety of reasons, including. Chapter 13

Taking your business to the next level can mean. Chapter 14

Here are some strategies to take your brand to the next level. Chapter 15

Product enhancements can help businesses reach new customers and penetrate new markets. Chapter 16

Here are some strategies to take your brand to the next level. Chapter 17

Here's a summary of our discussion: Chapter 18

Here are 12 business ideas from Chapter 1.

Here's an introduction to what it takes to start each of these businesses, along with key considerations and final thoughts on pursuing entrepreneurship:

Freelance Writing:

G Startup: Low Capitai, Primaria Computer, and Skills
G WatchOutFor:Fiercecompetitionand
irregular income.
G Final Thoughts:Freelance Writing Offers
flexibility and potential for success if
You create a powerful brand and market it effectively.
Consulting Services:

G Startup: Low to moderate capitation for
certifications and marketing.
G WatchOutFor:Initiaiciientacquisition
can be challenging.
G FinaiThoughts:Consulting Cabe
with expertise and dedication, but building a solid base takes
time.

Teaching or tutoring:

G Startup:Lowcapitai,maini materials
and marketing.
Watch out for seasonal demand and the potential need for
certification.
G FinaiThoughts: Teaching or tutoring can be fun and
profitable with the right approach.

Photography Services:

G Startup:Moderate To High Capital For
quality equipment.
Watch out for fierce competition in the industry.
G Fine Thoughts:Photographyoffers
creative opportunities, but success
requires skill and effective marketing.

Landscaping and Gardening:

G Startup:Moderatecapitaifortooisand
equipment.
G WatchOutFor:Weather-dependent
income.
G. FinaiThoughts: steady demand, but the physical nature of
the work should be considered.

E-commerce Store:

Startup: Varies by niche, i.e., for
dropshipping.
Watch Out For: Intense Competition and Ongoing Marketing
G FinaiThoughts:Scaiabiebutrequires
Careful niche selection and marketing
Handmade Crafts:
G Startup: Moderate Capitaiformateriais and Oniine Store
Setup
G WatchOutFor:Market Saturation
some niches.
G Final Thoughts:0ffers creative
expression, but competition can be
tough.

Event Planning:

Startup: moderate capacity for marketing and networking
G Watch out for: stress at times,
requires strong organizational skills.

Dear Mr. or Miss Untropernewer, Venture
Capitalist.
I appreciate your interest in starting a business with limited
capital. Here are 12 business ideas, each
1. Freelance Writing: Utilize your writing skills to offer content
creation services.
online. Success odds are moderate to
high, depending on your niche and marketing efforts.

2.ConsuitingServices:Leverage Your
seeking expertise to advise businesses or individuals.
Success odds can vary but are generally favorable if you
have a strong reputation.
3.TeachingorTutoring:Offeroniine
courses or tutoring in your area of
expertise. The odds are good.

G FinaiThoughts:Goodpotentiaiinareas
with a vibrant event scene.

Home-Based Catering:

G Startup: Moderate-to-High Capacity for IICs and Equipment
G Watch0utFor:Strict regulations and
seasonal demand.
G FinaiThoughts: high profit potential, but primary skills and
competitiveness are crucial.
Social Media Management:

G Startup: low capital for marketing and a computer
G Watch0utFor:Constantiearningand
adaptation.
G Final Thoughts:Growing Demand For
social media expertise. Dropshipping Business:
G   Startup:Lowcapitaiforanoniinestore.
G Watch0utFor:Thinprofitmarginsandimited controi

especially if you can demonstrate your
expertise. 4. Photography Services: Start a photography
business, focusing on events, portraits, or commercial work.
The odds of success can be high with the right skills and
marketing.
5. Landscaping and Gardening: Use your gardening hobby to
offer landscaping and gardening services. Success odds are
moderate, with demand varying by location.
b.E-commerce Store: Seii Products
online through platforms like Etsy or Shopify. Success odds
depend on your product selection and marketing strategy.
7. Handmade Crafts: Create and Sei
handmade crafts and goods. Success odds vary but can be
favorable with unique, high-quality items.
8. Event Planning: Utilize your organization's skills to plan
and coordinate events. The odds of success can be high with
strong networking and marketing.

G FinaiThoughts: Potential for Success with Careful Niche
Selection and Marketing

Virtual Assistant Services:

G Startup: Low-Capita Website and Marketing
Watch Out For: Competitive price, Time
Management is crucial.
G Final Thoughts:High Demand With The
right skills and marketing strategy.
In conclusion, starting a business involves careful planning,
dedication, and adaptation to challenges. Success is
attainable, but it often requires hard work, patience, and the
ability to learn from failures. Pursuing your entrepreneurial
dreams can lead to both personal and financial fulfillment,
making it a rewarding journey for those willing to take
The leap.

9.Home-BasedCatering:Offer Catering
services for Small events and gatherings. Success odds
depend on your culinary skills and demand.
10.SociaiMediaManagement:Manage
social media accounts for businesses
The odds of success are good if you understand social media
trends and algorithms.
11. Dropshipping Business: Start an ecommerce business
without holding inventory. Success odds depend on your
product selection and marketing strategy.
12.VirtuaiAssistantServices:Provide
administrative support remotely. The odds of success are
good with strong organizational skills and time management.

The Best Business For You To Start Depends
on your skills, interests, and the current market conditions in
Columbus, Ohio. It's essential to conduct thorough market
research, create a solid business plan, and consider your
financial resources before making a decision.

I hope this information helps you in your entrepreneurial
journey. If you require more details on any of these business
ideas or assistance with specific aspects, please feel free to
ask.

Chapter 2

Taik asked about the capital each of these businesses would
require. How many employees it would take to make the
business run. Give data on the daily cost of each of these
businesses.
Here's a breakdown of the capital required, the number of
employees needed, and the daily operation costs for each
business idea:

Freelance Writing:
G Capitai:Low. Primarily, it involves a computer and an

internet connection.
G Employees:Typically One-person
operation.
G Daily Costs:Minimal,maine
utilities and internet fees.
Consulting Services:

G Capitai: low to moderate, depending on certifications and
marketing.
G Empioyees:0ftenasoioventure,
but you may hire assistants as your business grows.
G DaiiyCosts:0Ficespace,
marketing, and occasioned travel expenses.
Teaching or tutoring:
G Capitai:Low. Materials and marketing expenses may vary.
G Employees:Usuaiiyaone-person
operation.
G Daily Costs:Minimal, Mainly Marketing, and Transportation
Photography Services:
G Capitai:Moderate To High For
quality camera equipment.
G Employees:Typically work out, but assistants may be hired
for larger projects.
G DaiiyCosts:Photography
equipment maintenance and
marketing expenses. Landscaping and Gardening:

G Capitai:Moderate. Expenses include tuition, equipment,
and
marketing.
G Employees:May Require Smaii

team, especially for
projects.
G Daily Costs:Fuel,maintenance ,
and marketing expenses.
E-commerce Store:
G Capitai:Varies Widely Niche.
Can be done with dropshipping,
higher with inventory.
Employees: In the beginning, it can be a one-person
operation, but you may need assistance with growth.
G-Daylry Costs: Website Hosting, Marketing, and Potential
Inventory Costs
Handmade Crafts:
G Capitai: Moderate Formateriais and Online Store Setup
G Employees:Usuaiiyaone-person
operation, but you may hire him
during peak times.
G Daily Costs: Materials,packaging, and marketing expenses
Event Planning:

G Capitai: Moderate. Expenses for marketing, networking,
and office
space.
G Empioyees:0ftenasoioventure,
but you may need additional staff.
for Larger events.
Daily Costs:Marketing, Transportation, and Other Expenses
Home-Based Catering:
GE Capital:Moderate To High For
licenses, kitchen equipment, and marketing.
G Employees:Dependsonthescaie
of your catering. You may need a
small team.
Dairy Costs:Ingredients, Kitchen Utilities, and Marketing
Expenses
Social Media Management:
G Capitai:Low.Mainly Marketing

expenses and a computer.
G Employees:Initially,a one-person
operation, but you can scan more characters.
Daily Costs: Marketing and
software subscriptions.
Dropshipping Business:

G Capitai: Low for an online store and marketing
Employees: You may be a one-person operation, but you
may need help with customer service.
G Daily Costs: Marketing and occasional customer service
expenses
Virtual Assistant Services:
G Capitai:Low. Main expenses for a website and marketing
G Employees:initially one-person
operation, but you can scan more characters.
Daily Costs: Marketing and
software subscriptions.

Please keep in mind that the capital requirements, number of
employees, and daily costs can vary greatly based on your
specific circumstances, location, and the scale at which you
want to operate your business in Columbus, Ohio. It's
essential to create a detailed business plan to accurately
estimate these factors.

Chapter 3

Here's some information with a brief description and an
assessment of their potential for success: Information on the
startup costs and success rates for each business idea:
Freelance Writing:
G StartupCosts:Minimal.Maine
expenses for a website, computer,
and internet access.
G SuccessRate: Moderate to High If You Build Strong
Portfolio and

market your services effectively.
Consulting Services:
Startup costs are low to moderate, depending on your niche.
May involve legal and consulting
fees.
Success Rate: A favorable person with expert ideas has a
solid base but can be challenging at first. TeachingorTutoring:
Startup costs: low materials and
Marketing expenses may vary.
Success Rate: Good if you find a niche with demand and
establish a reputation.
PhotographyServices:

G StartupCosts:Moderate To High
for quality equipment and software.
G Success Rate: high potential,but competition is fierce.
Success
It depends on your skills and
marketing.
Landscaping and Gardening:
G StartupCosts:Moderate. Expenses for transportation,
equipment, and marketing
G SuccessRate: moderate with consistent demand but can
be weather-dependent.
E-commerce Store:
Startup costs vary widely by niche. Can be lower with
dropshipping and higher with inventory.
G SuccessRate:Moderate,high
dependent on niche selection and marketing efforts.
Handmade Crafts:
G StartupCosts:Moderate For
material and online store setup.

G Success Rate: Moderate due to market saturation in some niches.
Event Planning:
G StartupCosts:Moderate. Marketing and networking are crucial.
G SuccessRate: Good in areas with a vibrant event scene, but can be
stressful.
Home-Based Catering:
Startup Costs: Moderate to High for IICs, Kitchen Equipment, and Marketing
G Success Rate: High Potential, but Success Depends on Circular
Skiiis and locai demand Social Media Management:
Startup Costs:Low.Maintenance Mainly expenses.
G Success Rate: Moderate to High Due to the Growing Importance of
social media.
Dropshipping Business:
Startup Costs: Low for an online store and marketing

G SuccessRate:Moderate. Thin profit margins, but potential for success with niche selection.
Virtual Assistant Services:
Startup Costs:Low. Main expenses for a website and marketing
G SuccessRate:Moderate To High
with the right skills and marketing
strategy.

Success rates can vary widely based on individual effort, market conditions,and location. It's crucial to conduct thorough research, create a business plan, and be prepared for challenges in any entrepreneurial endeavor.
Please note that these estimates are general guidelines and can vary significantly.
on your specific circumstances and location

Chapter 4

Here's a breakdown of the capital required, the number of employees needed, and the daily operation costs for each business idea:

Freelance Writing:
G Capitai:Low. Primarily, it involves a computer and an internet connection.
G Employees:Typically One-person operation.
G Daily Costs:Minimal, maintenance utilities, and internet fees
Consulting Services:
G Capitai: low to moderate, depending on certifications and marketing.
Employees: often as needed,
but you may hire assistants as
Your business grows.
G Daily Costs: office space, marketing, and occasional travel expenses
Teaching Or Tutoring:
G Capitai:Low. Materials and
Marketing expenses may vary.

Employees: Use a one-person operation.
G Daily Costs: Minimal, Mainly Marketing, and Transportation
Photography Services:
G Capitai: Moderate to high for quality camera equipment.
G Employees:Typicaiiyasoio endeavor, but assistants may be hired for larger projects.
G Daily Costs: Photography

equipment maintenance and
marketing expenses. Landscaping and Gardening: G
Capitai:Moderate. Expenses include transportation,
equipment, and marketing.
G Employees:May Require Small team, especially for larger
projects.
G Daily Costs: Fuei, maintenance,
and marketing expenses.
E-commerce Store:
Capitai: Varies widely by niche.
Can be done with dropshipping,
higher with inventory.

Employees: In the beginning, it can be a one-person
operation, but you may need assistance with growth.
Daily Costs: Website Hosting, Marketing, and Potential
Inventory Costs
Handmade Crafts:
G Capitai: Moderate Formateriais and Online Store Setup
Employees: Usually a one-person
operation, but you may hire him
during peak times.
G Daily Costs: Materiais, packaging,
and marketing expenses. Event Planning:
G Capitai: Moderate. Expenses for marketing, networking,
and office
space.
Employees: often needed,
but you may need additional staff.
for Larger events.
Daily Costs: Marketing, Transportation, and Other Expenses
Home-Based Catering:

GE Capital:Moderate To High For
licenses, kitchen equipment, and marketing.
G Employees:Depends on the situation
of your catering. You may need a
small team.
Daily Costs: Ingredients, Kitchen
utilities, and marketing expenses.
Social Media Management:
Low maintenance, marketing expenses, and a computer
G Employees:Initially,a one-person
operation, but you can study with
more clients.
Daily Costs: Marketing and
software subscriptions. Dropshipping Business:
G Capitai: Low for an online store and marketing
G Employees:initially one-person
operation, but you may need help.
with customer service.
Daily Costs: Marketing and
occasional customer service expenses.
Virtual Assistant Services:

G Capitai:Low. Main expenses for a website and marketing
G Employees:initially one-person
operation, but you can scan more characters.
Daily Costs: Marketing and
software subscriptions.

Please keep in mind that the capital requirements, number of
employees, and daily costs can vary greatly based on your
specific circumstances, location, and the scale at which you
want to operate your business in Columbus, Ohio. It's
essential to create a detailed business plan to accurately
estimate these factors.

Chapter 5
Here's a concise summary of what it takes to start each of these businesses, along with key considerations and final thoughts on pursuing entrepreneurship:
Freelance Writing:

G Startup: Low Capitai, Primaria Computer, and Skiis

Watch Out For: Fierce Competition and Irregular Income
G FinaiThoughts: Freelance writing offers flexibility and potential for success if
You create a powerful brand and market it effectively.

Consulting Services:

G Startup: Low to moderate capitation for certifications and marketing.
G Watch0utFor:Initiaiciientacquisition
can be challenging.
G FinaiThoughts:Consulting Cabe
With expertise and dedication,
But building a solid base takes time.

Teaching or tutoring:

G Startup:Lowcapitai,maini materials
and marketing.
Watch out for seasonal demand and the potential need for certification.
G Final Thoughts:Teaching Or Tutoring
can be fulfilling and profitable with the
right approach.

Photography Services:

G Startup: Moderate-to-High Capacity for Quality Equipment
G Watch0utFor:Fiercecompetitionin
the industry.
G Fine Thoughts:Photographyoffers
creative opportunities, but success requires skill and effective
marketing.

Landscaping and Gardening:

G Startup:Moderatecapitaifortooisand
equipment.
G WatchOutFor:Weather-dependent
income.
G. FinaiThoughts: steady demand, but the physical nature of
the work should be considered.
E-commerce Store:

Startup: Varies by niche, i.e., for
dropshipping.
G Watch0utFor:Intensecompetitionand
ongoing marketing.

G Final Thoughts:Scabie but requires careful niche selection
and marketing efforts.

Handmade Crafts:

G Startup: Moderate Capitaiformateriais and Online Store
Setup
G Watch0utFor:Market Saturation
some niches.
G Final Thoughts:0ffers creative

expression, but competition can be
tough.

Event Planning:

G Startup:Moderatecapitaiformarketing
and networking.
Watch Out For: Stress, at times, requires strong
organizational skills.
G FinaiThoughts:Goodpotentiaiinareas
with a vibrant event scene.
Home-Based Catering:

G Startup: Moderate-to-High Capacity for IICs and Equipment

G WatchOutFor:Strictreguiationsand
seasonal demand.
G FinaiThoughts: high profit potential, but primary skills and
competitiveness are crucial.

Social Media Management:

G Startup:Lowcapitaiformarketingand
a computer.
G WatchOutFor:Constantiearningand
adaptation.
G Final Thoughts:Growing Demand For
social media expertise. Dropshipping Business:
G Startup:Lowcapitaiforanoniinestore.
G WatchOutFor:Thinprofitmarginsand
limited control.
G FinaiThoughts: Potential for Success with Careful Niche
Selection and Marketing
Virtual Assistant Service

G Startup: Low-Capita Website and Marketing
Watch out for: In competitive situations, time management is crucial.
G Final Thoughts:High Demand With The
right skills and marketing strategy.

In conclusion, starting a business involves careful planning, dedication, and adaptation to challenges. Success is attainable, but it often requires hard work, patience, and the ability to learn from failures. Pursuing your entrepreneurial dreams can lead to both
personal and financial fulfillment, making it a
rewarding journey for those willing to take
the leap.

The analysis for each of the startup businesses details the profits and losses they can expect. Chapter 6

1. Freelance Writing:

- **Profit Potential:** Freelance writing can be profitable once you build a solid client base. Rates vary, but experienced writers can earn a competitive income.
- **Losses:** Initially, income might be irregular. You may encounter unpaid invoices or periods with fewer assignments.

2. Consulting Services:

- **Profit Potential:** High earning potential, particularly in specialized niches Rates vary but can be substantial for experienced consultants.
- **Losses:** Initial client acquisition may be slow, leading to lower income at the start.

3. Photography Services:

- **Profit Potential:** High potential for profit, especially for event and commercial photography. Rates vary widely but can be lucrative.
- **Losses:** Startup costs for quality equipment can be substantial. A competitive market may initially require aggressive marketing efforts.

4. Landscaping and Gardening:

- **Profit Potential:** Profit margins can be good, and steady demand exists for landscaping and gardening services.
- **Losses:** Initial investment in tools and equipment, along with potential seasonality, can impact profits.

5. Home-Based Catering:

- **Profit Potential:** High profit potential with a strong client base Catering for events and special occasions can be particularly lucrative.
- **Losses:** Compliance with regulations and initial expenses for licenses and equipment can affect initial profitability.

6. Virtual Assistant Services:

- **Profit Potential:** Scalable with the right clients Rates vary but can be competitive.
- **Losses:** Initial client acquisition and competition can make it challenging to generate consistent income.

It's important to note that the profit and loss potential for each business varies depending on factors such as location, market demand, pricing strategy, and individual effort. A well-researched business plan, effective marketing, and the ability to manage costs are key to maximizing profits and minimizing losses. Additionally, it's common for new businesses to operate at a loss initially as they build a client base and establish their presence in the market. Careful financial management and planning are crucial for long-term success in any entrepreneurial venture.

There are a number of different types of startup analysis that can be used to compare different businesses.
Some of the most common types of analysis include: Chapter 7

- Competitive analysis:

    This type of analysis looks at the competition in a

particular market and identifies the strengths and weaknesses of each competitor. This information can be used to develop strategies to compete more effectively.

- Customer analysis:

  This type of analysis looks at the target market for a business and identifies their needs and wants. This information can be used to develop products and services that meet the needs of the market.

- Industry analysis:

  This type of analysis looks at the overall industry in which a business operates. This information can be used to identify trends and opportunities that can be exploited by the business.

- SWOT analysis:

  This type of analysis identifies the strengths, weaknesses, opportunities, and threats facing a business. This information can be used to develop strategies to capitalize on opportunities and mitigate threats.

By conducting a thorough startup analysis, businesses can gain valuable insights that can help them improve their chances of success.

Here are some specific examples of analysis that can be used to compare different startups:

- A freelance writer could compare their rates, experience, and portfolio to those of other freelance writers in their niche.
- A lawn care company could compare their prices, services, and customer reviews to those of other lawn care companies in their area.
- A restaurant could compare their menu, prices, and atmosphere to other restaurants in their neighborhood.

By conducting this type of analysis, startups can get a better understanding of their competition and how they can position themselves to succeed.

Parts of a Business Plan, Chapter 8

Depending on the complexity of your business idea, a business plan can be as short as a page or as long as a thick, data-packed document. No matter how simple or complex, every business plan should have at least a few key parts:

- **An executive summary**, or a top-level outline of everything in the business plan.

- **A business description**, including your company's structure, industry, value proposition, background information, and both short- and long-term business objectives.

- **A market analysis** that evaluates where your business stands in relation to competitors, target customers, and industry trends

- **A description** of your products or services.

- **Financial projections** like pricing and sales strategy, profit goals, and investor details

- **An operational overview** laying out the logistical hows of your business, including logistics, distribution, and production plans.

Ignore this cost at your peril. Chapter 9

While it's not a line on the profit and loss statement, it is important for business owners to be intentional.

about identifying and quantifying opportunity costs in their business. Opportunity costs show up in a number of ways. The most common example is a business owner who spends time on tasks or areas of the business that are not the best use of their time or talent.

While they may be saving on the cost of hiring for or outsourcing that work, they are actually costing themselves more by tying up their time and often doing the job poorly. Another example is businesses that take on clients who aren't the best fit.

This may cause the reallocation of resources, which in turn slows growth or dilutes the company brand.

Growth will happen faster when opportunity costs are addressed.

Creating sound systems and processes is essential to finding anomalies in costs and revenues and refining profitability.

Point of sale systems; inventory management; and bookkeeping practices, processes, and

Procedures will help ensure you can find out what's wrong faster. It's often easy for business.

Owners who have been in business for a while rely on qualitative data and therefore neglect quantitative

data that is easily found. For example, a retailer may think that a particular product is flying off the shelves, but after

Looking at the numbers, you realize that's not the case.

Develop a strategic plan. Chapter 10

Develop short-term goals: quarterly, semi-annual, or annual, and create a plan that will help

you reach those goals. Make sure your plan considers the resources you may need: cash, people,

equipment, inventory, and additional operating costs, and make sure the end result will be a service.

or products that customers are looking for.

Set the metrics you will use to monitor your progress towards attaining that goal.

Adjust your plans as needed based on how close or far you are from your goal. If you aren't meeting your goal,

Determine why you are not meeting it. Is it a lack of resources? Is marketing not working?

Are you targeting the right customer segment?

To take your business to the next level, you can try these strategies:

- Set goals: define what you want to achieve with your business.

- Focus on customers: Build customer loyalty by providing great customer service.

- Embrace technology: Use business technology to reach customers in new ways.

- Hire the right people. Find employees who are eager for a second chance.

- Boost productivity: Increase productivity without increasing working hours.

- Reduce risks. Be adaptable and think ahead.
- Invest in yourself and your business.

- Get advice: Get professional advice from a business coach.

To take your business to the next level, you can try these strategies:

- Set goals: define what you want to achieve with your business.

- Focus on customers: Build customer loyalty by providing great customer service.

- Embrace technology: Use business technology to reach customers in new ways.

- Hire the right people. Find employees who are eager for a second chance.

- Boost productivity: Increase productivity without increasing working hours.

- Reduce risks. Be adaptable and think ahead.
- Invest in yourself and your business.

- Get advice: Get professional advice from a business coach.

- Learning new technologies: making sound decisions that can help save time, money, and other resources
- Attracting better leads: having enough people and processes to handle the leads
- Keeping up with changing technology: making better decisions and saving money, time, and other resources
- **Generative AI is experimental**. Information quality may vary.

Business growth is the increase in a company's size, revenue, market share, and profitability. Chapter 11
- over time. It can be achieved through a variety of means, including:

- Expanding into new markets
- Developing new products or services
- Increasing sales
  - Business growth is a function of the business lifecycle, industry growth trends, and the owners desire for equity value creation.

There's no universal formula for calculating business growth since each company is a unique ecosystem. However, the Harvard Business Review suggests that most companies should grow at a rate of between 10% and 25% per year.

Signs of company growth include customer count, headcount, customer happiness, and product maturation.

Some businesses may experience additional stages of growth, such as a shakeup or market introduction.

Business growth is typically measured by either increasing revenue or profitability. The growth rate is calculated by dividing the difference between the current period value and the previous period value by the previous period value. The result is expressed as a percentage.

Here are some other metrics that can be used to measure business growth:

- Conversion rate

- Return on investment (ROI)
- Customer lifetime value (LTV)
- Customer acquisition cost (CAC)
- Return on ad spend (ROAS)
- Percentage of revenue from new vs. existing customers
- Website traffic
  - The compound annual growth rate (CAGR) is a useful calculation for summarizing growth over longer time frames, like 5, 10, or 20 years.

Businesses should measure growth on a continuous basis. Keeping monthly or quarterly records can give owners insight into how their business is expanding.

Business growth metrics are used to measure a company's performance and profitability. Some important business growth metrics include:

- Customer acquisition cost (CAC): compares the number of leads to conversion rates to determine the cost of attracting a customer.
- Revenue churn measures the recurring income lost due to customer churn or downgraded subscriptions.
- Annual recurring revenue (ARR) estimates the revenue a company is expected to generate each year.
- Sales revenue indicates how well a business is performing.
- Customer retention is the percentage of customers retained by a company over a specific time period.
- Gross margin: The higher the gross margin, the more a company earns per sales dollar.
- Taking your business to the next level can mean:

  - Scaling your operations: having the right systems and processes in place to support a larger business
  - Having a financial plan: ensuring you have the resources to support your growth
  - Providing amazing service: Having high-quality products and services and constantly improving what you do

- Learning new technologies: making sound decisions that can help save time, money, and other resources
- Attracting better leads: having enough people and processes to handle the leads
- Keeping up with changing technology: making better decisions and saving money, time, and other resources

Business growth. Chapter 11

is the increase in a company's size, revenue, market share, and profitability over time. It can be achieved through a variety of means, including:

- Expanding into new markets
- Developing new products or services
- Increasing sales

Business growth is a function of the business lifecycle, industry growth trends, and the owners desire for equity value creation.

There's no universal formula for calculating business growth since each company is a unique ecosystem. However, Harvard Business Review suggests that most companies should grow at a rate of between 10% and 25% per year.

Signs of company growth include: Customer count, Headcount, Customer happiness, Product maturation.

Some businesses may experience additional stages of growth, such as a shake-up or market introductBusiness growth is traditionally measured by increasing revenue or profitability. To calculate a company's growth rate, you can use the formula:

- Subtract the original value from the new value.
- Divide the result by the original value.

- Multiply the result by 100 to turn it into a percentage.

Some other metrics that can be used to measure business growth include:

- Conversion rate
- Return on investment (ROI)
- Customer lifetime value (LTV)
- Customer acquisition cost (CAC)
- Return on ad spend (ROAS)
- Website traffic

Businesses should measure growth regularly, such as monthly or quarterly. This can help owners ensure they are growing at a rate that meets their targets.

Business growth metrics. Chapter 12

are a way to track a company's performance and profitability. Some important metrics include:

Revenue churn

This metric measures the recurring income lost due to customer churn or downgraded subscriptions.

Annual recurring revenue (ARR)

This metric estimates the revenue a company is expected to generate each year. It's calculated as the total revenue from existing customers in the last year.

Sales revenue

This metric indicates how well a business is performing. It's calculated as the number of sales multiplied by the price per sale.

Customer retention

This metric measures the percentage of customers retained by a company over a specific time period.

Gross margin

This metric measures how much a company earns for each sales dollar. It's especially important for starting companies.

Other important metrics include:

- Cash flow
- Customer satisfaction and loyalty
- Operational performance and productivity

Measuring business growth. Chapter 13 is important because it helps you understand where your business is and how fast it's growing. This information can help you:
- Mitigate risks

- Secure funding and expertise
- Understand if you need to make changes to improve results
- Make structural changes, like hiring new employees or purchasing new equipment

Some metrics that businesses can measure include:

- Revenue
- Customer acquisition
- Customer churn
- Customer engagement and retention

The type of business you run can affect how you measure success. For example, a charity might measure success by how many people they've helped

Growth management is important for the success of any business. It involves implementing strategies to help a business grow sustainably and profitably.

Growth is crucial for the long-term survival of a business. It can help a business:

- Acquire assets
- Attract new talent
- Fund investments
- Boost revenue
- Hire additional personnel
- Expand their offerings
- Acquire new customers
- Make their business more appealing to investors

- Survive unpredictable changes in the business ecosystem

Growth management is essential for companies of all sizes and industries, particularly SMEs, looking to expand and compete with larger organizations. However, if a business expands too quickly, it risks becoming unsustainable. Growth can put pressure on staff and resources, as well as financial and management structures.

Business growth can be beneficial for a variety of reasons, including. Chapter 13

- Taking advantage of opportunities
- Broadening offerings
- Lower costs due to economies of scale
- Greater market dominance
- Greater buying and bargaining power
- Ability to mitigate commercial risks

Here are some ways to grow a business:

- Attract new customers
- Engage existing customers
- Pursue new distribution channels
- Grow through acquisition
- Increase revenue
- Increase the number of employees
- Increase the number of customers

A growth-focused owner can be the driving force behind a company's expansion. Other managers and employees need the motivation and expertise to push a company to expand.

Business growth can be measured by tracking sales figures, total revenue, or average transaction value. Ported

Taking your business to the next level can mean. Chapter 14

- Scaling your operations: Having the right systems and processes in place to support a larger business
- Having a financial plan: Ensuring you have the resources to support your growth
- Providing amazing service: Having high quality products and services, and constantly improving what you do
- Learning new technologies: Making sound decisions that can help save time, money, and other resources
- Attracting better leads: Having enough people and processes to handle the leads
- Keeping up with changing technology: Making better decisions and saving money, time, and other resources

Other tips to take your business to the next level include:

- Finding new ways to reach customers
- Building and retaining a skilled team
- Maximizing your profit margins
- Building professional connections
- Using social media the right way

To grow your business to the next level, you can try these strategies:

- Set goals: Define what you want to achieve with your business.

- Focus on customers: Build customer loyalty by providing great customer service.

- Embrace technology: Use business technology to reach customers in new ways.

- Hire the right people: Find employees who are eager for a second chance.

- Boost productivity: Increase productivity without increasing working hours.

- Reduce risks: Be adaptable and think ahead.
  - Invest in yourself: Invest in yourself and your business.

- Get advice: Get professional advice from a business coach.

Other strategies include:

- Finding new ways to reach customers
- Building and retaining a skilled team
- Maximizing profit margins
- Building strong cybersecurity
- Making strategic acquisitions

Here are some strategies to take your brand to the next level.
Chapter 15

- Be human and approachable: Connect with influencers and people who share your values.
- Enhance the user experience: Make the brand fun and develop products that help other industries and consumers.
- Give more than you take: Share your knowledge, industry trends, and insights.

- Optimize your website: Improve your brand image by making your site faster and lowering your bounce rate.
- Find your courage: Show the world who you are and what you stand for with conviction and confidence.
- Build brand loyalty: Keep existing customers loyal and passionate about your brand.
- Use content creators: Generate content that can be shared on your own channels.
- Be consistent: No matter how long it takes.
- Get internal alignment: On brand identity.

A successful brand is more than just a combination of colors and logos. It's all about your reputation and the impression you make on customers.

To take a product to the next level, you can try these strategies:

- Research: Conduct market research, customer interviews, and product trend analysis.
- Categorize: Make it easy for customers to find what they're looking for. Include every detail and authentic photos.
- Focus on customers: Set goals, keep track of progress, and learn continuously.

- Use technology: Keep up with technology trends and use AI to analyze sales data and customer demand patterns.
- Use creative strategies: Get your brand noticed and visible to customers.
- Use time management: Spend 60% of your time on tasks that add value to your business.

Other strategies include:

- Using a complaint box
- Testing before investing
- Using partnerships
- Keeping up with technology trends
- Looking for low-cost, high-impact marketing tactics

Product enhancement can involve changing a product's design, materials, manufacturing process, or packaging. The goal is to make the product more appealing to consumers, which can increase sales.

Here are some ways to improve a product:

- Add new features and functionalities
- Improve the quality of the product
- Improve the appearance
- Create different versions of your product

- Change the form of the product
- Improve the production process
- Run small iterations
- Bring existing features up to date

You can also improve a product in response to customer feedback or to address safety or quality concerns. You can use surveys and polls to gather feedback from customers. You can also engage customers in the development process, such as by getting them to participate in beta testing.

You can also run a competitive analysis to determine and prioritize the popular features among your competitors

Product enhancement can take many forms, including:

- Leveraging new technologies
- Extending product capabilities
- Improving product usability
- Improving product performance and scalability
- Making the product more customized to different users

Here are some examples of product enhancement:

- Some companies have upgraded to ceramic flat irons because they distribute heat more evenly
- Software companies often increase revenue by releasing updated versions of their products
- Netflix has adapted to changing customer trends and expectations to expand
- Apple has modified existing products and sold them into their existing market

Product enhancements can help businesses reach new customers and penetrate new markets. Chapter 16

They can also drive growth and increase market share.

Product enhancements are changes made to an existing product to improve its performance. The goal of product enhancements is to increase the value of the product, improve the user experience, and maintain a competitive advantage.

Product enhancements can take many forms, including:

- Leveraging emerging technologies
- Extending product capabilities
- Improving product usability
- Improving product performance and scalability
- Making the product more customized to different users

Product enhancements can also include changes to a website or app to improve KPIs such as conversion, engagement, or revenue.

Product enhancements are important for businesses because they:

- Keep products up-to-date
- Increase product quality
- Improve customer satisfaction
- Increase product competitiveness

The goal of product enhancements is to increase the value of the product, improve the user experience, and maintain a competitive advantage.

Product enhancements can take many forms, including:

- Leveraging emerging technologies
- Extending product capabilities
- Improving product usability
- Improving product performance and scalability
- Making the product more customized to different users

Product enhancements can also include changes to a website or app to improve KPIs such as conversion, engagement, or revenue.

Product enhancements are important for businesses because they:

- Keep products up-to-date
- Increase product quality
- Improve customer satisfaction

- Here are some strategies to take your brand to the next level. Chapter 17
-
- Be human and approachable: Connect with influencers and people who share your values.
- Enhance the user experience: Make the brand fun and develop products that help other industries and consumers.
- Give more than you take: Share your knowledge, industry trends, and insights.
- Optimize your website: Improve your brand image by making your site faster and lowering your bounce rate.
- Find your courage: Show the world who you are and what you stand for with conviction and confidence.
- Build brand loyalty: Keep existing customers loyal and passionate about your brand.
- Use content creators: Generate content that can be shared on your own channels.
- Be consistent: No matter how long it takes.

- Get internal alignment: On brand identity.

A successful brand is more than just a combination of colors and logos. It's all about your reputation and the impression you make on customers.

- increase product competitiveness

To take a product to the next level, you can try these strategies:

- Research: Conduct market research, customer interviews, and product trend analysis.
- Categorize: Make it easy for customers to find what they're looking for. Include every detail and authentic photos.
- Focus on customers: Set goals, keep track of progress, and learn continuously.
- Use technology: Keep up with technology trends and use AI to analyze sales data and customer demand patterns.
- Use creative strategies: Get your brand noticed and visible to customers.
- Use time management: Spend 60% of your time on tasks that add value to your business.

Other strategies include:

- Using a complaint box

- Testing before investing
- Using partnerships
- Keeping up with technology trends
- Looking for low-cost, high-impact marketing tactics

Product improvements can be minor or substantial. For example, a company that sells flat irons might upgrade to ceramic irons because they distribute heat more evenly. Another example is Microsoft replacing its MS-DOS with Windows, a more user-friendly operating system.

Product improvements can include:

- Making a product from higher quality materials
- Making a product more durable
- Making a product organic, healthier, and planet-friendly
- Making a product work twice as fast as other versions
- Adding new features

Product improvements can attract new customers and discover new ways to use the product. To improve a product, you can:

- Research your competitors
- Talk to experts
- Learn about your target audience
- Look at how your competitors have marketed their products
- Research your customers

Being a good boss involves a variety of skills, including.
Chapter18

Building trust: Trust is important for effective communication, employee engagement, and job performance.

Giving feedback: Provide constructive feedback in a kind and respectful way.

Inspiring employees: One-on-one time with employees should inspire them to do better and think outside the box.

Motivating employees: Skilled managers can motivate employees to work hard and stay loyal to the company.

Being generous: Employees want bosses to be generous with information, time, praise, and coaching.

Getting to know employees: Successful managers find ways to support their employees so they can produce their best work.

Teaching employees: Outstanding managers teach their team how to be better workers.

Being self-reflective: Being a good boss involves being self-reflective.

Resolving conflicts: Good bosses resolve conflicts thoughtfully and decisively.

Delegating: Good bosses are willing to delegate.

Communicating: Good bosses maintain communication with their staff.

Providing advice: Good bosses provide actionable advice and instructions.

Employee engagement is important for organizations because it can help improve work culture, increase productivity, and reduce staff turnover. Here are some ways to keep employees engaged:

- Provide resources
- Keep communication open
- Be clear with expectations
- Give regular feedback
- Improve based on feedback
- Host company events
- Express gratitude
- Encourage teamwork
- Recognize their hard work

Employee engagement can also help build better work and customer relationships, and impact

Great managers can engage employees by:

- Building relationships that go beyond work
- Meeting regularly with their team members
- Getting to know their employees
- Providing support, feedback, and recognition
- Letting employees make decisions
- Celebrating successes
- Focusing on strengths rather than weaknesses
- Providing opportunities for growth

Great managers understand that happy, engaged employees are more productive, stay with their organization longer, and contribute to a wider culture of commitment. They know that employees want purpose and meaning from their work, and want to be known for what makes them unique.

What qualities do bosses value most?

Here's are some qualities that make a great boss:
- Provides feedback.
- Supportive.
- Recognize efforts.
- Get to know employees.
- Makes work fun.
- Decisive.
- Is available for employees.
- Share credit with staff.

- Here are 18 strategies that truly work.
- **1.** **Be disciplined.** Most entrepreneurs are people of impulse, and most passionate people live by feelings. But those who understand and practice the art of discipline can channel those impulses into something of substance.
- **2.** **Know yourself.** Get feedback from others and learn as much as you can about how you come across. Then you can accurately target how you appear in a crowd and what you need to work on.
- **3.** **Be conscious.** Showing up consciously means always being on time, honoring your commitments, and being prepared. Nothing is more powerful than an individual acting out of a well-developed consciousness.
- **4.** **Be confident.** When you truly believe you can create what you envision, when

you're not afraid of the obstacles, that confidence will automatically make you stand out from the rest.

- **5.** **Practice listening.** Learn to truly listen–to work toward a deep understanding and hear what's being said beyond the words. You will stand out in any situation if you become a person who listens from the heart.

- **6.** **Cultivate emotional intelligence.** Too many otherwise smart people don't know how to manage their emotions or relate to others well. Emotional intelligence attracts people who are looking to connect with someone who has their act together and who's competent and capable.

- **7.** **Be response-able.** Be the kind of person who responds and remembers to follow through. Most people drop the ball and don't follow up. Respond to emails, calls, requests, and inquiries as soon as you can. You will stand out as a person who respects others and is accountable.

- **8.** **Lead with excellence.** Let people know that quality is a core value, that everything that you do you do with excellence. Leading with excellence prepares you to deliver high-quality work and makes you stand out as a professional.
- **9.** **Know your motives.** Why do you do what you do? How well do you know your purpose—your why? Knowing your motivation helps you keep going and makes you easy for others to relate to.
- **10. Take yourself seriously.** Being an entrepreneur, leader, or businessperson requires that you become a master at your craft. It means being competent at the things you do, constantly honing and developing your skills in every way possible. When you take yourself seriously, so do others.

- **11. Always be of service.** Being useful, being helpful is an important aspect of making a great impression. Show up with a spirit of empathy and something to give. An attitude of service makes people interested in what you have to offer.

- **12. Don't make everything about you.** Few things are more boring than a self-centered person. When you meet someone, make the conversation about them, not you. Be interested and engaged; ask questions and listen carefully.

- **13. Be kind to everyone.** Lots of people are only nice to those who can do something for them. Stand out by treating everyone as important and interesting—even those who can do nothing for you in return.

- **14. Be prepared.** When an opportunity turns up, the person who is ready and able to be part whatever needs to happen will always stand out.

- **15. Be a master collaborator.** Be a great team player. Make others look good and sound good. When you collaborate well, people remember how you made them feel—and when people feel good around you, you stand out.

- **16. Love yourself.** It has nothing to do with ego, but a confidence within you that elevates your relationships with everything else. You'll stand out by being modest but happy with who you are.

- **17. Be inspirational**. A passion for life attracts others to you. To stand out and inspire others, you first must be inspirational.

- **18. Make your life your message.** Make sure that everything you do—how you show up, how you act, what you say, what you do—is a reflection of who you are, so your character and spirit are consistent across every situation.

- Great things can happen when you set yourself up to be noticed in the right ways. Practice these tips and you'll not only stand out in the crowd but probably travel far beyond it.

To stay ahead of your competitors, you can try these strategies:

- Know your competitors: Conduct market research to understand how people respond to your products or services and how they respond to your competitors.
- Know your customers: Understand what matters to your customers and what makes them tick. These insights can shape your product development, branding, and marketing.
- Differentiate: Create a unique value proposition (UVP) that communicates what your company does that your competitors don't. Your UVP could be pricing, a niche product, or a unique brand story.
- Plan: Have a clear idea of the direction you want to take and brainstorm ways to stay ahead while catering to your customer base.
- Step up your marketing: Update your image and expand your offer.

- Target new markets: Look after your existing customers and target new markets.

While it's good to stay aware of what your competitors are doing, you should also focus on what you do.

Losing customers to competitors can have many reasons, including poor service, price increases, or a poor product. Here are some strategies to stop losing customers:

- Improve customer service: Prioritize customer service and respond quickly to messages.
- Build relationships: Develop relationships with customers by building trust and having honest interactions.
- Offer resources: Provide resources like product tutorials to help customers maximize their investment.
- Keep your word: Don't forget to call customers back or get on things right away.
- Invest in your brand: Advertise, market, and promote your brand to regain market share.
- Know your competition: Look at what your best competitors do.

- Be innovative: Be innovative.

Some other strategies include:

- Personalizing contact with customers
- Using email marketing to keep in touch
- Starting a loyalty or referral program
- Surveying your.
- If you are going to be a leader or hold a leadership position, there's one quality you absolutely require to be successful.
- You need to be a seeker.
- A seeker is someone who is always searching.
- Seekers bypass mediocrity and are not content to settle for the status quo.
- They search for excellence with integrity and character.
- To be a great leader, commit to seeking in everything you do:
- **Seek your true character.** Leadership grows from character. Don't be concerned with your reputation; instead seek to clarify

your character, because your character is what you truly are while your reputation is merely what others think you are. Seek your true character daily.

- **Seek your unique qualities.** Don't be trapped by the dogma of other people's thinking. Work to discover and develop your own unique gifts and qualities and let them lead you to the kind of contribution that only you can make.

- **Seek the truth.** Any form of dishonesty—distorting facts, false impressions, conscious misleading—harms your leadership. Work to discover the truth in every situation and speak always with honesty and candor.

- **Seek your own core values.** Change is inevitable in business, in events, in the culture, in the people around you. Through it all, hold firm to the unchanging strength of your core values. When you do, you can challenge yourself in tough times, be courageous in fearful times and make a difference when it matters.

- **Seek to trust and to be trusted.** Great leaders know there's nothing more important than creating trust. Trust should be central to everything you do and every relationship you enter into. Seek trust in every action and every word.

- **Seek a compelling vision.** As a leader, you are responsible for creating a culture in which people are inspired to work together toward something bigger than themselves. Seek your compelling vision so you can share it with those who will be with you on the journey.

- **Seek to share your knowledge.** All the knowledge in the world is of little use if you don't seek to share it and use it in ways that help others. Cultivate the skills that will help you better serve, teach, mentor and lead.

- **Seek forgiveness.** For many leaders the phrase "I'm sorry" doesn't come easily, but it is the leader who can apologize and seek forgiveness who has true power. Seek to let go of your own anger, move past what hurts and look to make things right.

- **Seek something bigger than yourself.** Living is about losing yourself to find yourself. The greatest rewards come when you seek a way to give of yourself. It's about bettering the lives of others, being part of something bigger than yourself and making a positive difference.
- What you do as a leader is one thing, what you seek as a leader is another.
- When you are a seeker you are constantly looking for new ways of doing old things, trying to find how you can make things better not only for you but for everyone around you.
- If you can have just one quality as a leader, be a constant seeker.
- **Lead from within:** As a leader, your main concern is not to avoid failure or to live in

success but to always seek more meaning,

growth and development.

Chapter 19

Here's a summary of our discussion and the best way forward
for anyone looking to start a business:
We've explored various business ideas, each
with its own startup requirements, potential for success, and
challenges. The best way forward for aspiring entrepreneurs
involves the following steps:
IdentifyYourPassionandSkiiis:
Choose a business that aligns with your
interests, skills, and expertise Your passion will be a driving
force in your entrepreneurial journey.
Conduct thorough research: investigate the market conditions
in Columbus, Ohio, and the specific industry you're interested
in.
Understand your target audience, competition, and potential
demand. CreateaDetaiiedBusinessPian:
Develop a comprehensive business plan.
pian that outlines your business Goals, financial projections,
marketing

strategy, and operations. This document will serve as your roadmap. Secure Adequate Capital: Assess the startup costs and ongoing expenses of your chosen business. Ensure you have sufficient capital or access to funding sources to cover these costs.

Building a Strong Online Presence: In today's digital age, having a professional website and a strong
Online presence is crucial for marketing.
and attracting customers.

Network and Market Effectiveness: Networking with peers and potential customers is essential. Effective marketing strategies, both online and offline, will help you reach your target audience.

Adapt and Learn: Be prepared for
challenges and setbacks along the way. The ability to adapt, learn from mistakes, and continuously improve is critical to long-term success.

Monitor Finances Closely: Keep a close eye on your business finances. Budget wisely, track expenses, and ensure your revenue exceeds your costs.

Seek Professional Guidance: Don't hesitate to seek advice from mentors, industry experts, or business
consultants. Their insights can be
invaiuabie. Stay committed and persistent. Entrepreneurship can be demanding.
but staying committed and persistent in
Pursuing your dreams is essential.
Success often comes to those who
persevere.

Evaluate and Adjust:Reguiariyevaiuate
Your business's performance and
Adjust your strategies as needed.
Flexibility and the willingness to change course when

necessary are keys to
long-term success.

Remember that starting a business is a journey filled with
both challenges and opportunities. It requires dedication and
hard work.
work, and a willingness to learn. However, the
The potential for personal and financial fulfillment makes the
endeavor worthwhile. Embrace your entrepreneurial spirit and
take the first steps toward making your business dreams a
reality.

Here's a concise conclusion of what it takes to start each of
these businesses, along with key considerations and final
thoughts on pursuing entrepreneurship:

Freelance Writing:

Startup: low capital, primarily a computer, and skills
• Watch out for fierce competition and irregular
income.
• Final Thoughts: Freelance writing offers flexibility and
potential for success if you build a strong portfolio and market
effectively.

Consulting Services:

Startup: low to moderate capital for certifications and
marketing
*Watch Out For: Initial client acquisition can be
challenging.
Final Thoughts: Consulting can be effective with expertise
and dedication, but building a client base takes time.

Teaching or tutoring:

Startup: low capital, mainly materials and marketing.
• Watch out for seasonal demand and potential needs.
for certification.
• Final Thoughts: Teaching or tutoring can be fulfilling.
and profitable with the right approach.

Photography Services:

• Startup: Moderate to high capital for quality
equipment.
• Watch out for fierce competition in the industry.
• Final Thoughts: Photography offers creative opportunities,
but success requires skill and effective marketing.

Landscaping and Gardening:

• Startup: Moderate   capital   for   tools   and
•equipment.   Watch out for: weather-dependent
•income.
Final Thoughts: steady demand, but the physical nature of
the work should be considered.
E-commerce Store:

Startup: Varies by niche; low for dropshipping
• Watch out for intense competition and ongoing
marketing.
• Final Thoughts: Scalable, but requires careful niche
selection and marketing efforts.

Handmade Crafts:

• Startup: Moderate capital for materials and online
store setup.
• Watch out for market saturation in some niches.
• Final Thoughts: It offers creative expression, but
competition can be tough.

Event Planning:

• Startup: Moderate capital for marketing and networking.
*Watch Out For: Stressful at times, requires strong organizational skills.
Final Thoughts: There is great potential in areas with a vibrant event scene.

Home-Based Catering:

• Startup: Moderate to high capital for IICs and equipment.
Watch out for: strict regulations and seasonal demand.
Final Thoughts: High profit potential, but culinary skills and compliance are crucial.

Social media management:

Startup: low capital for marketing and a computer
• Watch out for constant learning and adaptation.
• Final Thoughts: Growing Demand for Social Media Experience

Dropshipping Business:

Startup: low capital for an online store
• Watch out for thin profit margins and limited control.
• Final Thoughts: Potential for success with careful niche selection and marketing

Virtual Assistant Services:

• Startup: low capital for a website and marketing

Here's a concise conclusion of what it takes to start each of these businesses, along with key considerations and final thoughts on pursuing entrepreneurship:

Freelance Writing:

Startup: low capital, primarily a computer,and skills
• Watch out for fierce competition and irregular income.
• Final Thoughts: Freelance writing offers flexibility and potential for success if you build a strong portfolio and market effectively.

Consulting Services:

Startup: low to moderate capital for certifications and marketing
*Watch Out For: Initial client acquisition can be challenging.
Final Thoughts: Consulting can be effective with expertise and dedication, but building a client base takes time.

Teaching or tutoring:

Startup: low capital, mainly materials and marketing.
• Watch out for seasonal demand and potential needs.
for certification.
• Final Thoughts: Teaching or tutoring can be fulfilling.
and profitable with the right approach.

Photography Services:

Summary of our discussion and the best way forward for anyone looking to start a business:

We've explored various business ideas, each with its own startup requirements, potential for success, and challenges. The best way forward for aspiring entrepreneurs involves the following steps:

Identify Your Passion and Skills: Choose a business that aligns with your interests, skills, and expertise. Your passion will be a driving force in your entrepreneurial journey.
Conduct Thorough Research: Investigate the market conditions in Columbus, Ohio, and the specific industry you're interested in. Understand your target audience, competition, and potential demand.
Create a detailed business plan. Develop a comprehensive business plan that outlines your business goals, financial projections, marketing strategy, and operational plans. This document will serve as your roadmap.
SecureAdequateCapital: Assess the startup costs and ongoing expenses of your chosen business. Ensure you have sufficient capital or access to
funding sources to cover these costs.
Build a Strong Online Presence: In today's digital age, Having a professional website and a strong online presence is crucial for marketing and attracting customers.
Network and Market Effectively: Networking with peers and potential clients is essential. Effective marketing strategies, both online and offline, will help you reach your target audience.

Adapt and learn: Be prepared for challenges and setbacks along the way. The ability to adapt, learn from mistakes, and continuously improve is critical to long-term success.
Monitor finances closely. Keep a close eye on your business's finances. Budget wisely, track expenses, and ensure your revenue exceeds your costs.
Seek Professional Guidance: Don't hesitate to seek advice from mentors, industry experts, or business consultants. Their insights can be invaluable.
Stay Committed and Persistent: Entrepreneurship can be demanding, but staying committed and persistent in pursuing your dreams is essential. Success often comes to those who persevere.
Evaluate and Adjust: Regularly evaluate your business's performance and adjust your strategies as needed. Flexibility and the willingness to change course when necessary are keys to long-term success.

Rememberthatstartingabusinessis Journey Filled With both challenges and opportunities. It requires dedication, hard work, and a willingness to learn. However, the potential for personal and financial fulfillment makes the endeavor worthwhile. Embrace your entrepreneurial spirit and take the first steps toward making your business dreams a reality.

summary of what it takes to start each of the six business ideas we discussed:

Freelance Writing: To launch a freelance writing career, leverage your writing skills and have minimal capital for a computer and internet access. Develop a strong

online presence, build a portfolio, and market your services effectively. Success comes with dedication and a continuous effort to secure clients and projects. Consulting Services:

Establishing a consulting business involves low to moderate capital for certifications and marketing. Your expertise is your key asset. Networking and building a client base take time, but dedication and a well-defined niche can lead to lucrative opportunities.

Photography Services: Starting a photography business requires moderate to high capital for quality equipment. Building a portfolio and engaging in effective marketing are crucial. Success in this competitive field comes from honing your skills, creativity, and commitment to ongoing learning.

Landscaping and Gardening: Launching a and gardening businesses involve moderate capital for tools and equipment. Market your services locally and offer seasonal maintenance packages. Success depends on your skills, hard work, and ability to manage a team for Larger projects.

Home-Based Catering: Home-based catering demands moderate to high capital for IICs, equipment, and marketing. Compliance with health and safety regulations is vital. The potential for high profit margins exists, driven by culinary expertise and effective marketing to attract clients.

VirtuaL Assistant Services:Creating A virtual assistant requires low capital for a website and marketing. Offering a range of administrative services can attract clients. Success in this competitive field comes with excellent organizational skills, time management, and adaptability to meet client needs.

Each of these business ideas offers unique opportunities and challenges. The key to success in entrepreneurship lies in

aligning your passion and skills with a well-researched business plan, diligent effort, adaptability, and a commitment to learning and growth.